Pebble® Plus

Animal Kingdom Questions and Answers

Reptiles
A Question and Answer Book

by Isabel Martin

Consulting Editor: Gail Saunders-Smith, PhD

CAPSTONE PRESS
a capstone imprint

Pebble Plus is published by Capstone Press,
1710 Roe Crest Drive, North Mankato, Minnesota 56003
www.capstonepub.com

Library of Congress Cataloging-in-Publication Data
Martin, Isabel, 1977– author.
  Reptiles : a question and answer book / by Isabel Martin.
      pages cm. — (Pebble plus. Animal kingdom questions and answers)
Summary: "Simple text and colorful images illustrate types of reptiles, including common characteristics, diet, and life cycle"—Provided by publisher.
  Audience: Ages 4–8.
  Audience: Grades K–3.
  Includes bibliographical references and index.
  ISBN 978-1-4914-0565-9 (library binding) — ISBN 978-1-4914-0633-5 (paperback) — ISBN 978-1-4914-0599-4 (eBook PDF)
  1. Reptiles—Miscellanea—Juvenile literature. 2. Children's questions and answers. I. Title.
  QL644.2.M3154 2015
  597.9—dc23   2013050614

Editorial Credits
Nikki Bruno Clapper, editor; Cynthia Akiyoshi, designer; Kelly Garvin, media researcher;
Katy LaVigne, production specialist

Photo Credits
Alamy: FLPA, 17, WILDLIFE GmbH, 19; Dreamstime/Chrispethick, cover, backcover; Shutterstock: apiguide, 15, EcoPrint, 9, Nagel Photography, 21, Rusty Dodson, 5, Ryan M. Bolton, 11, Sergey Uryadnikov, 7, Sonsedska Yuliia, 13, Zadiraka Evgenii, 1

Cover photo: tortoise; title page photo: green chameleon

Note to Parents and Teachers

The Animal Kingdom Questions and Answers set supports national curriculum standards for science related to the diversity of living things. This book describes and illustrates the characteristics of reptiles. The images support early readers in understanding the text. The repetition of words and phrases helps early readers learn new words. This book also introduces early readers to subject-specific vocabulary words, which are defined in the Glossary section. Early readers may need assistance to read some words and to use the Table of Contents, Glossary, Read More, Internet Sites, Critical Thinking Using the Common Core, and Index sections of the book.

Table of Contents

Meet the Reptiles

Slither, slither! A snake climbs up a rock. Snakes, turtles, alligators, and lizards are all reptiles. These animals come in many shapes, sizes, and colors.

mountain kingsnake

Do Reptiles Have Backbones?

Yes, reptiles have backbones.

A backbone is made up of

small bones called vertebrae.

The backbone is part of

a reptile's skeleton.

military dragon

Are Repiles Warm-Blooded or Cold-Blooded?

Reptiles are cold-blooded.

Their body temperature is

the same as their surroundings.

leopard tortoise

What Type of Body Covering Do Reptiles Have?

Reptiles have hard, dry skin covered with scales. Most reptiles molt, or shed their skin. New scales grow under the old ones.

scales

Texas horned lizard

How Do Reptiles Eat?

Most reptiles eat mice, frogs, and other animals. Alligators and snakes catch animals with their teeth. Some reptiles eat plants.

snake eating a frog

Where Do Reptiles Live?

Some reptiles live on land.

Other reptiles live in water.

You can find reptiles in rivers,

deserts, fields, and forests.

green iguana

How Do Reptiles Have Young?

Most female reptiles lay eggs.

Young reptiles hatch from the eggs.

Some reptiles give birth to live young.

panther chameleon
babies

Do Reptiles Care for Their Young?

Most reptiles do not care for their young. But crocodiles help their babies find water after they hatch.

Nile crocodiles

baby

mother

19

What Is a Cool Fact About Reptiles?

A python is a type of snake.

Some pythons have 400 vertebrae.

People have only 32 to 34 vertebrae.

Pythons bend and curl easily.

carpet python

Glossary

cold-blooded—having a body temperature that changes with the surrounding temperature

desert—a dry area with little rain

female—an animal that can give birth to young animals or lay eggs

hatch—to break out of an egg

molt—to shed an outer layer of skin; after molting, a new covering grows

scale—one of many small, hard pieces of skin that cover an animal's body

skeleton—the bones that support and protect the body of a human or other animal

surroundings—the things around something or someone

temperature—the measure of how hot or cold something is

vertebra—one of the small bones that make up a backbone

Read More

Arnosky, Jim. *Slither and Crawl.* New York: Sterling Pub., 2009.

Gregory, Helen. *All About Snakes and Lizards.* Wonder Readers. North Mankato, Minn.: Capstone Press, 2012.

Stewart, Melissa. *Snakes!* National Geographic Readers. Washington, D.C.: National Geographic, 2009.

Internet Sites

FactHound offers a safe, fun way to find Internet sites related to this book. All of the sites on FactHound have been researched by our staff.

Here's all you do:
Visit www.facthound.com
Type in this code: 9781491405659

Critical Thinking Using the Common Core

1. Why do the bodies of pythons bend easily?
(Key Ideas and Details)

2. Look at the pictures. What do all reptiles have in common?
(Integration of Knowledge and Ideas)

Index

Word Count: 182

Grade: 1

Early-Intervention Level: 15